INSIDE

Jeremy Cronin

RAVAN PRESS JOHANNESBURG

Published by Ravan Press (Pty) Ltd
P O Box 31134, Braamfontein 2017
Johannesburg, South Africa

First published 1983
Second impression 1987

ISBN 0 86975 172 7

Typesetting: Sandy Parker
Cover portrait: Mzwakhe Nhlabatsi
Cover design: The Graphic Equalizer

Printed by Blackshaws (Pty) Ltd, Cape Town

CONTENTS

I. INSIDE

Poem-shrike Page 3
Overhead is mesh 4
Walking on Air 5
Pollsmoor Sketches 15
Motho ke Motho ka Batho Babang 18
Thinks 19
Group Photo from Pretoria Local on the Occasion of a 4th Anniversary (Never Taken) 21
4 times 12 23
For Comrades in Solitary Confinement 25
Death Row 26

II. THE NAVAL BASE

I close my eyes 35
Like Jonah I recall 37
I cannot disclaim 39
Anointed. Let my nose 40
I wasn't allowed to be present 41

III. VENTURE TO THE INTERIOR

Prologue 45
Cave-site 46
Litany 47
Plato's Cave 48
Labyrinth I 49
Our land holds 50
If you're asking 51
Karroo – I 52
Karroo – II 54

The Ivory Trail 55
The River That Flows Through Our Land 57
To learn how to speak 58

IV. SOME UNCERTAIN WIRES

Granpa Kemp 61
Granma Kemp 62
My grandma had been getting old 63

V. LOVE POEMS

Invoking My Muse 67
Itchy with its 68
Tonight is an envelope 69
A Prayer In Search of Beads 70
Faraway city, there 71
Labyrinth II 72
as I remember 73
Chapman's Peak 74
Visiting Room 75
A Love Poem 76
I Saw Your Mother 77
Your Deep Hair 78
Eyelids 79
A bay scooped in Cape mountains 80
Somewhere inside here 81
Mirror 82

VI. ISIQUQUMADEVU

Isiququmadevu 85
White Face, Black Mask 87
I run a length of cotton twine 88

A grounded parachutist 89
Removed from the city 90
A Step Away From Them 91
In blue bluer-than-any-sea doeks 93
A Particular Day. 1975. 94
A Naming of Matches 95
Lullaby 96
A Tale of Why Tortoise Carries His Hut Upon His Back 98
Chameleon 100
Kwikkie 101
Clothes 102
Second Thoughts 103

I INSIDE

POEM-SHRIKE

For a body I've rolled up
inventory item six two three: one pair
socks short prisoner's European, dealt
for a tail
a tight hand from a scuffed
awaiting-trial playing card pack and added
50 finest quality
Rizla gummed
cigarette blaadjies scorched black.
From a prison cell floor comes this barred
light of your back, your
beak was bent
uptight for a week, your call with its
inner-side scratch I've rasped, your eyes
sharpened on the grindstone
down in the prison workshop, then dipped
in an old Koo tin of water from which they emerge
dripping light
nail sharp, tense, each as an i-dot.
I check your
hungry parts
over again, longing by longing then
out
over the high walls I launch you now . . .

sshrike!

Overhead is mesh,
To one side the morgue,
To one side the gallows wing, this
Is our yard

Into which a raggedy
By happenstance
Butterfly has flown,

Fluttering
Halfway to panic
Halfway to give a damn

Springtime has come.
The years flow into each other.
The struggle goes on.

WALKING ON AIR

Prologue

In the prison workshop, also known as the seminar room;

In the seminar room, sawdust up the nose, feet in plane shavings, old jam tins on racks, a dropped plank, planks, a stack of mason's floats waiting assembly, Warder von Loggerenberg sitting in the corner;

In the prison workshop, also and otherwise named, where work is done by enforced dosage, between political discussion, theoretical discussion, tactical discussion, bemoaning of life without women, sawdust up the nose, while raging at bench 4, for a week long, a discussion raging, above the hum of the exhaust fans, on how to distinguish the concept 'Productive' from the concept . . . 'Unproductive Labour';

In the prison workshop, then, over the months, over the screech of the grindstone, I'm asking John Matthews about his life and times, as I crank the handle, he's sharpening a plane blade, holding it up in the light to check on its bevel, dipping the blade to cool in a tin of water, then back to the grindstone, sparks fly: 'I work for myself' – he says – 'not for the boere';

In the prison workshop, with John Matthews making contraband goeters, boxes, ashtrays, smokkel salt cellars of, oh, delicate dovetailings;

Over the months, then, in the prison workshop, I'm asking John Matthews, while he works intently, he likes manual work, he likes the feel of woodgrain, he doesn't like talking too much, the making and fixing of things he likes, he likes, agh no, hayikona, slap-bang-bang, work for the jailers;

In the prison workshop, then, I ask John Matthews, was he present on the two days of Kliptown . . . 1955? . . . when the People's Congress adopted the Freedom Charter?

Actually

No he wasn't

He was there the day before, he built the platform

In the prison workshop, then, over the hum of exhaust fans, between the knocking in of nails, the concept 'Productive', the concept 'Unproductive Labour', feet in plane shavings, John Matthews speaks by snatches, the making and fixing of things he likes, though much, never, much you won't catch him speaking;

But here, pieced together, here from many months, from the prison workshop

Here is one comrade's story.

***

Born to Bez Valley, Joburg

into the last of his jail term
stooped now he has grown

In this undernourished frame
that dates back
to those first years of his life.

He was nine
when his father came
blacklisted home

From the 1922
Rand Revolt,
and there with a makeshift

Forge in their backyard
a never again to be employed
father passed on to his son

A lifelong
love for the making
and fixing of things.

From Bez Valley it was,
veiled like a bride in fine
mine-dump dust

He went out
to whom it may concern
comma

A dependable lad
comma
his spelling is good.

At fifteen he became
office boy at Katzenellenbogen's
cnr. von Wielligh

And President streets
where he earned: £1 a week,
where he learned:

* Good spelling doesn't always count.
* The GPO telegram charge is reckoned per word.
* A word is 15 letters max.
* You have to drop ONE *l* from Katzenellen-
bogen Inc or
HEAR ME BOY?! nex' time
YOU'S gonna pay extra one word
charge your bliksem self.

And the recession came
but he got a bookkeeping job
with Kobe Silk

On the same block
– John Edward
Matthews

Mondays to Fridays
on that same block
for 37 unbroken years until

The security police
picked him up . . . . But first
way back to the thirties.

WEEKENDS IN THE THIRTIES:
church and picnics

by Zoo Lake.

And later, deedle-deedle
– Dulcie, heel-toe,
his future wife

Whom he courted with
(he can still do it)
diddle-diddle: the cake-walk

And always
on Sundays it was
church and church.

And then to Kobe Silk
there came
a new clerk

Myer Chames by name
a short little bugger who talked
Economics at lunch-break

And Myer Chames talked
of all hitherto existing societies,
the history of freeman

And slave, lord, serf,
guildmaster, journeyman,
bourgeois, proletarian and

In a word
John Matthews stopped
going to church.

His name got inscribed

inside
of a red party card.

He'd sell Inkululekos down by
Jeppestown
Friday nights

While the bourgeois press wrote
RUSSIA HAS GONE SOFT ON HITLER
He learnt to fix duplicators and typewriters.

He was still selling
Inkululekos in 1943
when even the bourgeois press wrote

RED ARMY HAS BROKEN
BROKEN
THE BACK OF HITLER

In the year 1943 – born
to Dulcie and John
a daughter

Their first child
first of seven.
And now

Into the last months
of his 15 years
prison term

At nights in his cell
he peeps down at his face
in a mirror

In a mirror held low, about
belly-height,
wondering how he'll seem

To his grandchildren
from down there
next year when he comes out.

But that's later . . . back
to 1950
The Suppression of Communism Act

Membership becomes a punishable crime.
But laws only
postpone matters – somewhat.

There were still duplicators to fix
and typewriters to mend
through the 50s

Passive Resistance, the Congress Alliance,
Defiance Campaign, Pass Burnings, Bus
Boycott, Potato Boycott, the Women's
March, the Treason Trial, the Freedom
Charter, until

Until 1960: the massacre
Sharpeville
and Langa.

And people said: 'Enough,
our patience, it has limits' . . . and so
it was no longer just typewriters and duplicators
to mend.

A man would come to the backyard and whisper:
30 ignitors.
And John Matthews would make 30, to be
delivered to X.
And a man would come in the dead of night
These need storing comrade, some things
wrapped in waterproof cloth.
TERRORISTS BOMB POWERLINES
He would read in the bourgeois press, or
MIDNIGHT PASS OFFICE BLAST
He'd sigh a small sigh
—Hadn't been sure
Those damned ignitors would work.

Finally.
1964.
After a quarter century in the struggle

A security police swoop
and John Matthews was one
among several detained.

White and 52
so they treated him nice.
They only made him stand

On two bricks
for three days
and three nights and

When he asked to go to the lavatory
they said:
Shit in your pants.

But the State needed witnesses

So they changed their tune.
Tried sweet-talking him round.
Think of your career
        (that didn't work)
Think of the shame of going to jail
        (that thought only
        filled him with pride)
You really want kaffirs to rule?
        (like you said)
Think of your wife
        (Dulcie. Dulcie.
         7 kids. Dulcie.
         She's not political at all).

And there they had him.
On that score he was worried, it's true.
And they promised him freedom.
And they pressed him for weeks on end
Until finally he said:

Okay, agreed.

– But first I must speak with my wife.

Barely an hour it took them to find
and rush Dulcie Matthews
out to Pretoria Jail.

Then looking nice, because they let him shave, let him comb his hair, looking nice then, chaperoned by smiling, matrimonial policemen, shaven and combed, John Matthews got led out to his wife, and holding her hand, they let him hold her hand, he said

– Do you know why they've brought you?
And she said
– I do.
And he said
– Dulcie, I will never betray my comrades.
And with a frog in her throat she replied
– I'm behind you. One hundred percent.

So back they hauled John Matthews then and
there,
back to the cells,
that was that, then, but
all the way down the passage
toe-heel, heel-toe, diddle-diddle
ONE HUNDRED PERCENT
I mean, he was high
off the ground, man.

He was walking on air.

POLLSMOOR SKETCHES

I
It's never too late
For tattooed tears
Trane implies
With purple tear-drops
That stream down his cheek

Skin deep.

II
Las' time I getta ten years
But ony I pusha fife.
You wants to know why?
Ees beecause I no shtupid.
For eenstance, I polishing in da boeb
Deesa peeg, he come, he shtand over me
He say: 'Hey Portugoose,
Why you no polisha clean?'
                    I theenk:
FUCKA YOU!
                (I say
nothingk.)

III
The pay's kak
The prisoners give bek
And today my name's
AAAAAAAgterhek!
AAAAAAAgterhek!
That's me
Ting ting fok kak bek
I'm a turnkey.

IV

I'll shoot down Vorster any day of the week.
Hey kommie, you get me a gat
And I'll get you a boer
You bleddy cocksucking, kaffir loving,
Communis jew, I'll donner you up,
So pally, in your golden chains of friendship
Will you count me as a link?
So bra, will you see me right?
Jail's a shit sandwich
And every day we get a bite.

V

Listen man, I'm in boeb
For something
I hardly didn't do.

Course I knew Braam Fischer.
He tune me one day straight:
– Psssssssss
Hulloa Ginger.

VI

'*. . . in this epic theatre the actor does everything to make himself perceived standing between the audience and the event he portrays . . . .*'

– Brecht

Kom, kom, kom, kom, kom, kom, you donders,
Stand two-two, two-two, two-two!
For a head count and thumbprint check.
– Johannes Stephanus Februarie!
Gives a small stylized skip.
– Ja, o.b.
(Ou baas worn short with long use)

And begins his casual sideways shuffle, in caricature
of haste.

He rolls exaggerated thumbs in ink,
And with all the care of Albrecht Dürer
Prints them, tenderly.
In his hair he wipes off ink
As he slips back with head bowed and
Panache to his place in line.

There is,
Between Johannes Stephanus Februarie
And submission,
This epic gap.

MOTHO KE MOTHO KA BATHO BABANG
(A PERSON IS A PERSON BECAUSE OF OTHER PEOPLE)

By holding my mirror out of the window I see
Clear to the end of the passage.
There's a person down there.
A prisoner polishing a doorhandle.
In the mirror I see him see
My face in the mirror,
I see the fingertips of his free hand
Bunch together, as if to make
An object the size of a badge
Which travels up to his forehead
The place of an imaginary cap.
          (This means: *A warder*).
Two fingers are extended in a vee
And wiggle like two antennae.
          (He's being watched.)
A finger of his free hand makes a watch-hand's arc
On the wrist of his polishing arm without
Disrupting the slow-slow rhythm of his work.
          (*Later.* Maybe, later we can speak.)
Hey! Wat maak jy daar?
          – a voice from around the corner.
No. Just polishing baas.
He turns his back to me, now watch
His free hand, the talkative one,
Slips quietly behind
          – *Strength brother,* it says,
In my mirror,
          A black fist.

THINKS . . . .

Fish yes, not flesh nor fowl
here in this woolless world

Of the public aquarium's many
after hours, see

Off the top of my head
a stream of bubbles

That rises, that billows
above me, inside it

Is written:
THINKS dot-dot-dot

And no
word of a lie

Here in the tanks
of the public aquarium's

Filter green
iridescent mineral waters

Where always the time
seems like after hours

Where the looks of the guards
have surely departed

Leaving on glass
dot-dot-dot

Just
the prints of their stump-noses.

GROUP PHOTO FROM PRETORIA LOCAL ON THE OCCASION OF A FOURTH ANNIVERSARY (NEVER TAKEN)

An uprooted tree leaves
        behind it a hole in the ground
But after a few months
You would have to have known
        that something grew here once.
And a person's uprooted?
Leaves a gap too, I suppose, but then
        after some years . . . .
There we are
        seated in a circle,
Mostly in short pants, some of us barefoot,
Around the spot where four years before
When South African troops were repulsed before
                                                        Luanda
Our fig tree got chopped
        down in reprisal. – That's Raymond
Nudging me, he's pointing
At Dave K who looks bemusedly
Up at the camera. Denis sits on an upturned
Paraffin tin. When this shot was taken
He must have completed
        17 years of his first
Life sentence.
        David R at the back is saying
Something to John, who looks at Tony who
Jerks his hand
        So it's partly blurred.
There we are, seven of us
        (but why the grinning?)
Seven of us, seated in a circle,
The unoccupied place in the centre

stands for what happened
Way outside the frame of this photo.
So SMILE now, hold still and
click
I name it: Luanda.
For sure an uprooted tree
leaves behind a hole in the ground.
After a few years
You would have to have known
it was here once. And a person?
There we are
seated in our circle, grinning,
mostly in short pants,
some of us barefoot.

4 times 12
first thing in the morning is 48
. . . 48, I think what Engels said
about freedom being
the understanding of necessity
take away 6 is
. . . 42 more weeks, what'm I saying? MONTHS!
I want to shout
up into my mirror
from today I've only got
exactly
42 MORE MONTHS!
But you know
along this corridor we live
only in some ways
according to the same time
when we count other people's victories for instance
as our own
(which they are).
But there're those other times
parcelled
in separate
brown paper packets.
A time that walks in circles.
A time that flattens itself
incredibly thin
disappears
into the backs of mirrors
or drips from the taps.
When I first came to jail
some of my comrades had served
thirteen years –
drop by drop, they've been inside now
since before the armed struggles
in Mozambique and Zimbabwe

had even begun.
                                        I lie in bed
picturing myself
stepping out
in a new set of clothes
with a brown paper packet
– letters
seven years of letters
under my arm
                                        – in 42 months' time
when some of these comrades
                                        (counting
                                        Mozambique, Angola, Zimbabwe,
                                        . . . perhaps Namibia by then)
                                                        might
STILL be inside.

FOR COMRADES IN SOLITARY CONFINEMENT

Every time they cage a bird
the sky shrinks. A little.

Where without appetite –
you commune
with the stale bread of yourself,
pacing to and fro, to shun,
one driven step on ahead
of the conversationist
who lurks in your head.
You are an eyeball
you are many eyes
hauled to high windows
to glimpse, dopplered by mesh
how-how-how long?
the visible, invisible, visible
across the sky
the question mark – one
sole ibis flies.

DEATH ROW

I

The first we hear is this tremendous
cajoling laughter.

Ten minutes later, above our cells
Squeak-squeak-squeak, across the catwalk
Walks an unfamiliar warder.

It's three fokken terrorists – he says,
Not grasping, yet,

Who we are.
They're impossible, man. A person
Can't do
Nothing with them.

Johannes Shabangu.
David Moise.
Bobby Tsotsobe.

Having
Skipped the country
trained in diverse parts
slipped back clandestinely
Dug
diggers of the earth
residers of holes underground.
Sons of the soil
breath to be swallowed
breath swallowed by the night
In the night
darker than plain dark
and all so quiet

Sappers
Soweto's sons
stalkers
Who blew up
Sasol 2 by Secunda
Uncle Tom's Hall
Booysens, the cop shop
Dube line
likewise a place
near Malelane
Caught
Caught in a shoot-out
captured at Matola
strung upside down
Probed without days
in a night
in a river of needles
The clammy hood
choke hold
a year without season
For months
your bodies probed
months long until

finally you were led
unbowed into court
and charged
all three
with high treason.

Now nine months already, brothers
You've been sitting
On death row.

II
What concerning C section
can I tell you?

What down here could be different
from B section?

A section? Or from wherever
it is inside this slaughterhouse
they've just randomly
shifted you from?

Listen . . . two walls to the left.
A garden – I think,
from where this sound
leaks in.
A guinea-hen's call – we've been told,
glass on glass
a pocketful of marbles weeping
deep in her throat, but don't ask

On Wednesday mornings
almost every other week,
another, a staggered sound
like bioscope seats flapped
back. What's that!? Don't

Ask me, brothers, I

. . . Perhaps I didn't hear.

III
Of course we never get to speak,
As such, to each other.
We're still fifty yards, one corridor,

Many locked locks apart.

Nkosi sikelel', we try singing, at night.
Us down here, to you,
Three condemneds, along there.

Morena . . . we whiteys sing,
Mayibuye iAfrika, and muffled
Far-off chortling, you guys
Call back: *Encore! Encore!*

IV
Then it's you singing slow
Antiphonal phrases,
Three tongues floating over
        That audible
Drop which gathers,
The words thrumming in your
Throats, brothers,
        About which
Some Wednesday morning
        Three nooses will go.

        One voice leading:
Arrraaise ye, high up,
Everynight,
        Deeper, two in the chorus:
Prisoners from your slumbers
Called and
        To boil or
Respond like a
Ripple like a
Lurch like a
        Ukuhlabelela
is to

Glow like a
Growl like a
Glow like a
Boil like a
Bean stew like a
Ripple like a
Bus queue weaves like a
Moves like a
Stalks like a
Moves like a
Fighter
Ukuhlabelela
Three voices
Called or
Moise
Combine or responding
Tsotsobe
Weaving
Shabangu
In and
Voices
Each other
Around of, sliding
Into each night's
Finale, all three
Three now
As one: *Tha-a-a*
Inta
nasha – na – ale
yooonites tha
hooman
reisssss. a-MAAA
– ndla ! longleev
sisulu-mandela-tambo
LONGleev! LONGleev!

shouted *longleev!*
Your voices, brothers
Down these concrete
Corridors of power.

II THE NAVAL BASE

I

I close my eyes, and it's the sea's
entering soft foot, through
97 98 99 one
HUNdred! and call COMing!
across the streamlet
with its wild cat prints
through the port jackson scrub,
I check the beach, the old jetty,
and now into the house:
the wardrobe, pantry, under the beds.
These all being the finite number
of places a five-year-old
kid would hide, nose pinched
to stop his sneeze – the point
being not to be found
too soon,
nor ever to hide
where you wouldn't hear
my feet closing in, despite the precautions
stepped up in these last years,
as my feet approach, I could say:
I have come
just to troll
for mackerel from the pier's end, but who
would believe that
now? With you
in there, your nose pinched
hidden in the deepest ignorance
of the bulldozers moving on the zinc camp,
of the trek fishermen group area'd
out for the submarine pens,
as my feet approach, something
moves with the sea's snuffling
in through the countless fish

tastes of its underwater salads, awash
in the half-forgotten house by the beach
amongst the feeders, its stone valves,
these almost empty rooms,
shell, scale, pelt,
in the armed white camp, behind
the newest precautions, and my feet
approaching w-a-r-m-e-r. Feet
stumbling in this undergrowth.
Me hiding in there, ears pricked up.
Me out here circling about. There is
between the two of us, in this
necessary space, nothing,
nothing that could be learned,
or forgotten now
by backing off.

II

Like Jonah I recall the darkness.
At ritual and appointed hours,
in cod liver oil my tongue
would be anointed.
A symbol weighed inside my head
An anchor fixed betwixt my legs.
Eaten, then excreted, these
my imagined rites of passage – Yes,
childhood weighs
an anchor in my head, like an unanswered question
bucking to start into the tide's
smack in a hundred off-beat
digressions the snoek boats gasp
uh! – uh! – uh! – uh! – throttling
at first light, at sixty
glottal stops the minute – Where?
Where do babies come from?

I ask a sea anenome.
It folds a secret
mouth in its mouth.
People get married – says my mother.
When you're older you'll learn – says my father.
And the snoek boats go
uh! – uh! – uh! – uh! – uh!
Through a world charged with half hints
warmed with buckscent and
the wildest pelargonium, the mountain puts
a tentative toe in the sea.
In mid-bay a seal proffers
two dozing nostrils and
one laconic flipper. Where
do babies come from?

In winter the rains wash down
tennis balls from the coloured quarters on the hill.
I'd find them, Moses-like
in our streamlet's reeds.
Under my jersey I place them,
snuggled to my belly, in winter
when I'd whisper
into Jenny Brown's brown ear.
– *You STUPID!* she says.
Jenny Brown my parents' maid
– *Only women can make lighties.*
        – she laughs.

III

I cannot disclaim that string-thin, five-year old boy
with big ears and bucked teeth from thumbsucking
late,
who woke to dockyard hooters on mornings of
mackerel-green sea
that cast up sea-eggs, argonauts, unexplained white
rubber balloons.
A soft sea full of cutting things, of sharkstooth,
barnacles, and ultra marines.
Who polished with envy and Silvo his pa's ceremonial
sword.
Who dreamt of mama and the ocean's lap-lap,
and that one day the tide would ride out,
yes ride oh right out, uncovering bedclothes.
That boy, that endless earache, who knew at five,
because learnt by heart, the naval salute, the sign of
the cross,
the servant's proper place, and our father who art.
– This five-year old boy, this shadow,
this thing stuck to my feet.

IV

Anointed. Let my nose be now attentive.
Anointed, the waters of that sky,
The fish oil factory, and the acre
Just beyond.

Anointed is the wind that slicks back
And smooths down forever
The wavelets of that bay

Where the gun carriage rattled,
And the slow march marched,
Where lowered was a widow into widowhood,
And the blank shots got fired
Blankly into air.

Let my nose be now attentive,
From the morning watch,
Even until night, from the first dockyard hooter

From the depths crying out, this dissolution in the wind,
Water, fish, oil, factory, and
The burial acre just beyond.

V

I wasn't allowed to be present when
delirious with pain he said
(I was told many times after)
– *Jeremy must play cricket,* spoken three times,
three times over, while his body writhed and wasted.

Thus my father passed on
his patrimony of aspiration.

He was thirty-four when he died.

During the war he'd sailed on convoys to Murmansk
and Archangel,
– slender evidence this, against all else, as I search
now
for retrospective conciliation, perhaps
because to this day his last inconsequences
still voyage up through his pain,
all night zig-zag in my torpedoed dreams stumps fly.

III VENTURE TO THE INTERIOR

PROLOGUE

Now in your cockpit
from your pilot's seat within
test the distant parts of this machine.
Take the tongue-tip and feel up
t-t-t-t-t
there, just
behind your upper front teeth
the ribbed shoal that runs back and up
to a solid arch of bone.
Beyond, slide along the soft velum's central crease
peeling back and back on your tongue's joy stick
until you touch
the stem from which depends
a strange
perhaps forbidden fruit aaaaah!
say aaaaah!
working the throttles of your glottis.
And now
to cool a while
let the tongue untwine
returning to its berth.
Let lip touch lip
hmmmmm, mmmmm.
Flick the switch to In
then Out: these
being the two prevailing winds.

Are all systems go?
– Good.
Then let flesh be made words.

CAVE-SITE

I want you
to prise carefully
sound
from sound
to honour by speaking
(and sometimes to discard)
to lift, cough,
breccia, rock, sediment
layer through layer
in this
mouth or
cave-site of word
root, birdbone,
shells of meaning
left in our mouths
by thousands of years of
human occupation.

LITANY

Out of the primal swamps
down the line of the mudfish
through the snake where your ways parted
after the hardening of the palate
you came
        to me o
            Amphibian Rose
tchareep grrrtch-grrrtch
            tchareeep tchareeep tchareeep
            Protrusible Shadow
            Tree of Tastebuds
kree-kree-kree-kree
        sssszzzz
            from this jungle of unmapped sounds
        you arise
            Elastic Denizen
            Abettor of Mastication
            Disporting Porpoise
            Friend to Deglutition
            Concavity turned Turtle
        sszzzzzzzzzzz (_________!)
            Convexity of Muscle
        you come
            whirrra – whirrra – whirrra – whirrra
                                    dove
            Love Scout
            Periscope of Pleasure
            Winged Breath
                                    you come
                                        bearing the leaves of speech

            Tongue!
O Ark of Language.

PLATO'S CAVE

. . . would they not assume that the shadows they saw were real things?

Imagine a chamber that's cave-like and runs
down and down underground,
and imagine
within this chamber
there are prisoners with strange anatomical names.
Each is fastened here or there
and enfolded in dark.

Suppose further that these prisoners are restless,
that they hoist the back of their tongue
to enclose a pocket of air, and then
with a quick downward stroke they make
!quagga!
painting a palatal click on the roof of their cave.

Or suppose, hearing snatches of news,
they are filled with a deep longing,
these prisoners who incessantly mimic
the sounds of their land
down in the blue-veined stopes
down in the very confines of their chamber.

Supposing all this,
do you think they'd assume
this shadow play was real?
That these prisoners could forget
the struggles of their brothers and sisters
there outside where these sounds
bathed in the daylight, may

someday, grow into words?

LABYRINTH I

from a blanket
– unpicked,
twined for strength,
balled for concealment,
taken out in the dead of night,
this cotton thread,
weighted with a comb
on its casting end, this
– is a cable.

blind guessing
on distance and angle,
the comb skating off
many times
from under the chink, tentative,
of my locked door, trailing
its cotton tail, lifeline
out, as it jigs
back at last to rebound
under my neighbour's
cell door, this
– is a cable.

a thread of contact
down which to pass
a meagre
well read, smuggled-in, month-old, scrap of
– newspaper.

Our land holds its hard
Wooden truths like a peach
A pip:
        Out at Athlone
By the power station
Over two cooling towers, the wind
Turns visible in its spoors.
Skin and bone, zig-zag,
Through the khaki bush
It hums, the wind tongues
Its gom-gom, frets a gorah,
In a gwarrie bush the wind,
So I fancy, mourns, thin
Thin with worries:
                Goringhaicona
Goringhaiqua Gorachouqua: sounds
Like at the back of our sky
Cicadas' songs ache: Hessequa
Hacumqua, like vocables swallowed
In frogs' throats: Cochoqua,
The names of decimated
Khoikhoin tribes – their cattle stolen,
Lands seized
As their warriors died
Charging zig-zag into musket fire,
Those warriors who've left behind
Their fallen spears that our land
Like a peach its pip
        Holds now:

This unfinished task.

If you're asking: whose land?
Under the pounding of wood, consider
Between the grinding conversations, stone to stone,
Where the sun gives up its vegetable holds,
How many centuries
Have been stirred into putu?

Whose land? – if you're wondering
It's no use telephoning. Stamp the earth
Ask among the bones
Where the frogs bring down
Rain on their own heads, and the earth
Chews, chews,
Like a pair of scissors never getting fat.

Grain's seed, grass, shrub's roots
Where the men's bones with their snuff pouches,
Women's bones with their porridge sticks, ask
There where lineage on lineage sits
Tucked in this earth.

KARROO I

Under this spreadeagled
sky, in flight a tickbird,
neck tucked up, looks
bronchitic; a lizard
gathers breath; stone lies on stone,
and the road, a chewed thong
through this buckhide,
breathless unscrunched land
so parched, words,
of birth difficult,
stick, agh, buck, kop, grab,
shrub, rock, klip,
stick, traveller, in the back of your throat.

With each generation, you said,
The entire race passes
Through the body of its womanhood
                              – Olive Schreiner,
along these Karroo tracks
dissecting truths
about men, God,
. . . women,
your plaits pinned up,
        chewing
on pieces of paper, and later
in London
you looked
into a microscope
at spermatazoa, looked
back to twelve flat stones
        O God consume my offering.
        O God, like Elijah to be licked
                up in a heavenly fire.

O God, this little thing so much desired.
And God was unmoved.
For was it not, fiction aside,
a little girl and a lamb chop
left uneaten?
Its fat, like spent seed
trickling down the side of a stone
beneath this African, this spreadeagled sun.
– O Olive Schreiner
ceaseless campaigner
against all oppressors,
jingoes, warmongers,
God, Rhodes, the British South Africa Company.
Sowing seeds, letters to meetings,
you were too unwell to attend:

I am glad
To hear of your meeting.
I am glad that in your meeting
Men and women are combined
Because men and women
Are the right and left sides of humanity.
I am especially glad that women workers are taking their place in this meeting
As the most poorly paid
Heavily pressed section of labour
It is necessary women workers
Should learn solidly to combine.
I hope your meeting
Will be large and successful – signed:
Olive Schreiner, your letters

still keep arriving.

KARROO II

Into some hypothetical hotel – The Grand,
or The Milner – night sifts through
your words, and an opened window.
From generation to generation
language trekking on
through each of our throats:
koppie, sheepkraal, koppie,
milkbush, the town location, this whole
spanned outscattering dusted
in moon track,
farmhouse, prickly pears,
the star leaking sky, touched
all with your improbable word: *ethereal.*

Lonely, lonely, lonely,
somewhere out there deep, Olive Schreiner,
into this night,
in a broken down shack
(not knowing
she'll stir the world yet)
is this small intense girl,
deep in her book,
black as the night:
your great-great granddaughter.

THE IVORY TRAIL

Along this wheel scar, down the Ivory Trail,
Behind my canines, in the dust of my throat
You can hear my ancestor,
The Great White Hunter:
    'Three thousand', he would growl,
    'and some two hundred and fifty odd,
    back in 1918, yep,
                my best year, grandson – a drought.'
He nods. Hawks. Gobs.
    – Black Ivory,
That's what he called
    The contract mine labour he recruited north of
                                        the latitude
    22 degrees south.
    My forbear who went
Renaming the sons of man,
For unless a man be born again
    Sockies, Sikkies, Fife, Fifteen, Knife,
    Gladstone, Wellington, Houtkop, Jim,
    Tickey, Flappies, Doek . . . .
Into those ultra-deep levels,
More than a mile below the surface of this earth,
Contracted into low-roofed
Chambers where they move
A quarter million tons of rock
In a single stope each month,
While the pressure like a smothered
Shout, builds and buckles
While the stress points
Shift until, as they say,

She bumps . . . .
Tread

Tread, tread ever so softly now, grandpa,
There's men down there,
From 1918, remember? – and still
Chewing earth.

THE RIVER THAT FLOWS THROUGH OUR LAND

A swift stream in the high mountains, dropping
dental, lateral
Clicking in its palate like the flaking of stone tools;
And a wide river that grazes the plains,
Lows like the wind in summer maize.
And a waterfall that hums through a turbine
And is whirled into light.

A river that carries many tongues in its mouth.

And a river that flows from times of peace,
And times of war when its fords became slippery,
A river that has bathed spears and bridal parties.

And a river that trickles
Down the worker's face.
The salt river that welds tomorrow forward,
Steel girder on girder and concrete.

This is the river that flows through this land.

To learn how to speak
With the voices of the land,
To parse the speech in its rivers,
To catch in the inarticulate grunt,
Stammer, call, cry, babble, tongue's knot
A sense of the stoneness of these stones
From which all words are cut.
To trace with the tongue wagon-trails
Saying the suffix of their aches in -kuil, -pan, -fontein,
In watery names that confirm
The dryness of their ways.
To visit the places of occlusion, or the lick
in a vlei-bank dawn.
To bury my mouth in the pit of your arm,
In that planetarium,
Pectoral beginning to the nub of time
Down there close to the water-table, to feel
The full moon as it drums
At the back of my throat
Its cow-skinned vowel.
To write a poem with words like:
I'm telling you,
Stompie, stickfast, golovan,
Songololo, just boombang, just
To understand the least inflections,
To voice without swallowing
Syllables born in tin shacks, or catch
the 5.15 ikwata bust fife
Chwannisberg train, to reach
The low chant of the mine gang's
Mineral glow of our people's unbreakable resolve.

To learn how to speak
With the voices of this land.

IV SOME UNCERTAIN WIRES

GRANPA KEMP

A flash of tarred wattle poles in the corners of the
eyes,
the only apparent movement through these dried flats
from the road.
Strange that wide spaces could have made
such a narrow mind – this is Granpa Kemp country,
and those, he would have said, are his poles.

Retired to a smallholding, mealie patch, chicken hok,
and a garage filled with used Firestone tyres,
he was guided, when I knew him, still by those
self-taught
headstrong maxims, and a spike in the pantry for the
bills.

Foreman of a polegang he had been
when they worked with post office cables to stretch
and peg out this land; he bothered to speak
a few bastardized words of Xhosa – for command,
while every new pole carried
the pulse of colonialism in its overhead wires.

Most of a lifetime he gave, lonely out there
as the loneliest pole they ever raised.
In the end his eyes were dried to pale blue,
glass caps, insulators on a cross-beam.

GRANMA KEMP

An electric device listens in my cell's walls –
it must have been a bit like this you felt
with those, what you called,
creepy crawlies, and the big sun besides.

To Humansdorp, brought back from the Great War
along with his unextracted shrapnel, you were
The English Bride.

Forty years on, still pale and transplanted, my
Granma Violet,
late afternoons I'd wait with a small boy's fascination
until, parasoled, behatted, watering-can in hand
carefully you'd tread, down kitchen steps
into Africa.

My grandma had been getting old, of course,
so my mother felt she should perhaps
some time pay the call
she'd been putting off for years.

Her telegram read:
ARRIVING THURSDAY NEXT STOP
SHORT VISIT
It was wired from Cape Town through to Humansdorp.

Four hours later, the sudden appearance of this
message made
my poor grandma's dicky heart stop
dead.

The ceremony was held over until Thursday next,
and of course, etc., in short
nothing more was said.

But oh yes, I remember those telegraph wires!

When I was five we made a trip to my grandparents
once
– both were still alive.
I didn't ask my mother then
had these place-names
(when she'd travelled away from her childhood
– but going the other way)
each marked just another hundred more miles
thankfully erased?

Listen between Cape Town
past shanty towns, up to the Boland,
over dried flats, the roadsigns, the Riviersonderend,
to those thin telegraph wires.

Do they still hum? Is it still liar, liar, liar, your nose
is as long as something beginning I spied
with my little eye riddled with too much road,
birdsperch that hums its quavering song: Ai,
Ai, the witbors kraai flies from here to Mosselbaai,
George,
Outeniqua, Tsitsikamma, Storms River gorge – this
nostalgia
is thicker than water, my family,
between generations is all space
half filled with childhood rhymes, joined
by some uncertain wires.

V LOVE POEMS

INVOKING MY MUSE

Suppose these lines
Were to try for her grin, being
Slightly ironic yet
Altogether serious, if you see
What I mean?

Suppose the dark times, of unmarked cars,
Of our half expecting an unwanted
Knock on the door.
Suppose
A room which I enter and something is hurriedly
Shuffled away . . . .

A pamphlet? An illegal pamphlet?
It might be because

I would like these lines to invoke
Suddenly from out of those times
With a certain facial expression
One eye closed to modulate the glare,
Her head sideways tilted, mouth wry,
The back of her forearm sweeps
Wisps away from her brow . . .

To be remembered in all this?

Partly, the light I've switched on, and
Partly: (SHIT MAN Jeremy, I almost thought you . . . .)

Her grin.

Itchy with its
sound of crickets
this night could be
        anywhere (almost)

        – But it isn't.

As the first watch warder
arrives in our passage

Two remote controlled doors opened
and clanged shut

Three manually operated grilles opened
and clanged shut

Five locks
        just the beginning
of what lies between us.

But my love
to be removed
jailed endorsed out banished
man from woman is

After all
nothing unusual in this

Our country, in these times
in this night full of crickets
when to say plainly:

        'I love you'
is also
a small act
of solidarity with all the others.

Tonight is an envelope
Into which I climb, sliding between its folds
The letter I, flesh made paper
Turning in half, then again
        sleeplessly over.
Never more than 500 words
One letter per month quota, I take
Three weeks at least to arrive.
After their reckoning of words, after the censors,
After the ink-check, code-check, comes
A rubber stamping.
Tonight is this envelope into which I slide
As the selfsame letter formed on my tongue
My tongue turned into paper – tonight perhaps
Taking off as no more than 500 words
In a bat of the lids, it's just
Possible to consider me as flying at last
As three week old words, behind the inside flap's
        Gummed
Touch to reach you.

A PRAYER IN SEARCH OF BEADS

As a child I learned
to follow blind the circular path
where the hand was guide to the tongue
each bead unlocked
its own particular prayer.

But now I have to hope
for some reverse palpability to emerge.
I close my eyes – fervently,
Un zip . . . Un zip I intone
fumbling with its sounds
as if I hoped to touch
in that word, bump, bump,
the tingling, the warm
rosary down your spine.

Faraway city, there
with salt in its stones,
under its windswept doek,

There in our Cape Town where
they're smashing down homes
of the hungry, labouring people
– will you wait for me, my love?

In that most beautiful,
desolate city of my heart
where if staying on were passive
life wouldn't be what it is.

Not least for those rebuilding
yet again their demolished homes
with bits of plastic, port jackson saplings,
anything to hand – unshakeably

Defiant, frightened, broken,
and unbreakable are the people of our city.

– Will you wait for me, my love?

LABYRINTH II

. . . and Ariadne, her beautiful erotic thread unwinding, guiding him in the stone darkness . . . .

(Yannis Ritsos)

I'm unravelled by day, at night
I weave now and weave
with the fading scent
of soap, following its thread down
to another time, another bed
to where a-hooked and kicking we
ssshh – wildeye, like
two katonkel, made love.

Or awoke, a-tangled
androgyn, twice-fourlegged:
– us and the bed.
Laden with scents of voyages made
of voyages still to become
its pine frame solid enough to take
a mattress of foam, being
not too wide, being
– just so.

It had sheets that knew creases,
a pillow once swollen,
in daytime it became
a settee, where the back
of a knitting needle purled
at my upper left arm
as you knit and knit
the far end of this twine.

as I remember
these things are ribbed:
a sanddune
untouched:
a fishing boat
on a slipway:
the roof
of your mouth.

CHAPMAN'S PEAK

The sea's break
from high up's a continuous shush . . . .

She's a wingbone.
Not the Atlantic,

Nor the Atlantic's
duffling fog up on a headland.

Stone. Nor ligament
of stone fibre. She's

not the wide
fall, the gulled float, the wheel, plunge

and squinny, or the wind's
persiflage where it goes

down to the wheeze and
scuttle by the seafringe. But

a wingbone. The deft
birdpoise in her hip.

VISITING ROOM

To admit light,
that's a window's vocation,
or a man to a wife
at this very place
where the wall becomes
for the briefest moments – a window,
shadowed by warders.
A glass plate, its sheer
quiddity, its coldness

forever between our hands.

A LOVE POEM

I write: She's like some unnamed succulent of the veld.
    She says: That's really flat.
But I'm trying to say it like I feel.
    Then you'd better think twice, she insists.

So I write:
    Skimming two dark pools, her eyes,
    her eyelashes are glistening dragonflies.

That's better, she says, but
Why all this delicate nature stuff? It wasn't
A flower that taught you how to drive.

I SAW YOUR MOTHER

I saw your mother
with two guards
through a glass plate
for one quarter hour
on the day that you died.

'Extra visit, special favour'
I was told, and warned
'The visit will be stopped
if politics is discussed.
Verstaan – understand!?'
on the day that you died.

I couldn't place
my arm around her,
around your mother
when she sobbed.

Fifteen minutes up
I was led
back to the workshop.
Your death, my wife,
one crime they managed
not to perpetrate
on the day that you died.

YOUR DEEP HAIR

Remember the mierkat's
footfall down the inner-sleeve of night,
under the milkbush, under the curdled
star clouds of galactic semen
spilled across the sky, you turned in sleep and
from your deep hair tumbled
aromatic buchu and the wide veld.

Three months now.
Scalp shaved,
you died, they say,
your head encased in wraps.

EYELIDS

They signalled quietly,
two flags of their own.
Down for refusal. Up in surprise.
Down again for laughter – each
eyelid was restless as five
workmen or a broom, all
touch and go, they'd stroke
along the surface of an eyeball.
As careful as
a teaspoon of light,
a pinch of salt, or a dark petticoat.
Who can forget how they'd unveil
– between blinks,
            through all tears –
an unbreakable strength.

A bay scooped in Cape mountains
down a hillside of vygies, and namaqualand
daisies, and a wooden bungalow that holds nights of
candles.
In alliekreukels are those eyes, a voice
indistinguishable from the dark cleft
where the freshwater spring sings arums and
watercress.
Listen to the breathing that moves
through the anchored kelp beds. Look
the duiker's low flight to Bellows Rock.
That is also her gaze. Many times.
And if you're there, read
in the margins of the tidewash, in the sandpiper's
prints
a lesson inscribed in forgetting – it is not.

Somewhere inside here
Like part of me still deeply alive
Behind the blocked orifices of a head cold
While out there everything merged
Into its winter
Into its smudge and Claremont's nose dripped . . . .
Drips on a window-pane
Named for a cosmonaut, Valentina the cat
Still orbits in her sleep
Before the electric heater's yellow coil
Yellow the straw mat
And a drying pair of tights
                    Tossed
Quick over the back of a chair . . . .

I still go there, I mean
A small room
Behind my eyebrows
                    – Out of the rain.

MIRROR

Hold my hand and step
into the mirror
between the cool perimeters
of its drowned amphitheatre, wade in
bellyheight . . . shoulder height . . . point blank
snorkel down to the past
below the waterbug that crinkles
the meniscus of time.
Swim behind these curtains of exhalation to where
suspended
our submerged years
hang like dark bamboos
their feet shackled to the water-bed
their heads
still recall the sun.

Now hold tight
as we swim back to the air, but always
. . . only your face stares out with its nose
pressed
against an impassable glass frontier.

VI ISIQUQUMADEVU

ISIQUQUMADEVU

Take care, it's said, lest your shadow
        crosses the deepest of pools.

You think
        that's only old superstitions?

You won't accept
        Isiququmadevu lives there.

Or even admit
        that pools in South Africa are swallowers.

Gigantic swallowers into which
        not only the heedless may plunge.

Here where a thin sky
        plummets through the catwalk

Between bars and mesh and
        into the tunnels of my eyeballs

Until with a nerve
        sprung faraway splash the sky lands

Blue. When I first came to prison
        I'd write about rivers

Now my poems
        are all about pools,

Pools and mirrors into which
        I've been slipping it seems

Into that retrograde self
    where imaginary maidens

Come down to bathe
    where the old pronoun,

I, the swimmer behind eyelids,
    Isiququmadevu dreams

Daylong . . . agh, of
    snatching their clothes.

WHITE FACE, BLACK MASK

Thoughts
    concerning the person
    named Who:
Who is naked beneath his clothes,
Who is black in the night,
Who is
    unwashed before his bath,
and you mustn't suck cents
    you never know
Who might have touched them last.
Who is mask.
Who is beyond
    mask, lock, yale, bolt, chain, electric alarm.
Who,
    son of Who,
Who's Who, when the dog barks
there also is Who.
Who peeps through windows.
Who desires my mother, without a pass.
Who wields
    a double-edged knife.
Who entertains
    my darkest
desires.
Who,
    a temporary permanent
sojourner in my dream's backyard.
Who walks through our night.
Who stalks our women.
Who looks at my sister
    with longing.
        Yes,
Who.

I run a length of cotton twine between my teeth
Or I consider the hedging reticent tentative forward
motion of an ant
With its two blind man's sticks
Tock-tock tock-tock
Feeling left and right
I feel like being in love – but with whom?
It's six o'clock I'm writing these words
About stretches of bare concrete that cast me
Into the infinity of small things
I've begun to observe most closely a spider in the
corner of my cell
You'd think in prison I'd empathise only with the ant
Trussed head and foot now in a web – but it's also
the spider
The spider, this intense alliance eight legs to a bobbin
– consider
How it swings on its toothedge how it trawls in the
currents
At six o'clock as I spin out
The interminable lines of a love poem to no-one
Tock-tock tock-tock
To no-one in particular - and now
As if at the edge of my poem

I sit
And I wait.

A grounded parachutist, he pulls the ripcord
of his pyjama pants, he hums
he's got the whole wide world in his hand.
he thinks of Ryle's distinction:
knowing how/knowing that.
In magazines
are lips that slide from 2-D faces
to fly towards his metal supper plate.

They find it difficult to think
in three dimensions – he hears
the radio say for explanation
why there're so few SA engineers
who're black – Jesus!
Lock a white boy up
a few years inside, you'll find him
knowing that/but not knowing
how there're three dimensions to a woman.

Removed from the city now I live
an exile from confirmation
in a thousand reflective plate-glass fronts,
in ten thousand human faces, out of habitat
I've shrunk.
But how once I moved on escalators!
City, I lived your vibrance, once,
I, multiplicand, you the power of ten.
Yet not yet beyond division, both,
simple and long.

Poet, I too have tasted the city,
your polyglot, cosmopolite, mankind city!
On escalators I have felt the thrum simultaneous
I was ascending, that one descending,
that person also was me.
Yet Walt Whitman this unity is not yet won.
Our essence the aggregate of social relations, I live
divided
from my city: my city
not yet
diversely one.

A STEP AWAY FROM THEM

There's a poem called that
by Frank O'Hara, the American,
it begins: *It's my lunch hour so I go*
for a walk . . . . I like the poem, sometime
I'll write it out complete, but just for now
I've got this OK Bazaars plastic packet
in my left hand, and my right
hand's in my pocket (out of sight),
how else to walk lunch hour
summertime Cape Town with
one gloved hand? And now
I'm going past The Cape Clog
– Takeaways, it says it's
The Home of The Original
ham 'n cheese – Dutch Burgers,
past the unsegregated toilets on
Greenmarket Square. A cop van's
at the corner. On a bench
3 black building workers eat
from a can of Lucky
Star pilchards. They're
in various shapes & sizes. It's a fact.
Though you'd think
post boxes'd be all
just one size. I'm sweating a bit,
heart pumps, mouth dry, umm
Gone one, I say slipping
past the Groote Kerk when
an Iranian naval sailor asks
What's the time? IRANIAN? – yessir,
it's 1975, the shah's
in place, the southeaster blows,
there're gulls in the sky,

two cable cars are halfway
up or down (respectively) and
outside the Cultural Museum
an old hunchback tries
to flog me 10c worth of unshelled
nuts. He's been here
since I was 15
trying to be Baudelaire, I'd maunder
round town watching women's legs, but now
I've only
eyes for postboxes and
my heart's in my packet: it's
one thousand
illegal pamphlets to be mailed.

In blue bluer-than-any-sea doeks, in rubber galoshes,
Arm over arm, three lunch-time pals,
Three dark women and their laughter

As opposite the cannery my train arrives
From many years back and
Slows into Woodstock station.

Three women eating lunch, glimpsed
From the window.
Salt light for laughter, galoshes
Studded with a cat's
Eyed blink in a myriad of pellicles.

Three women, six knowing hands
Fresh from, x the number,
Bodies of fishes.
In gutting and scaling there being, I'd guess,
No malice, nor any your equals.

Your hands planing cross-grain to the flesh,
Your galoshes collecting the soft milt
Spray of hake scales.
Into your tender propitious hands, sisters,
From the night parts of the seas, I commend
Lucky – all fishes.

ONE PARTICULAR DAY. 1975

The municipal bins stood
stock still at dawn on that day
strapped to their individual poles
present
present
present
they intone in my mind's ear
if only to confirm by the simplest
roll call of their names:
Vullis Blik – Hou U Stad – Keep Your City –
Clean – that this place was real, ditto –
the sound of metal to metal from the cargo
ships hove to, close by in the bay
and the freight train's ring-ting-ting
memento loitering in a place long since
it has left behind – yes,
yes, all this occurred
with the sky's opening up
between the even now of things past
and the not yet where
already the footstep
of what's to come sounds.
At dawn of that day, downtown
an elevator marked *Goods & Non-Whites* began
slowly to rise, by the bus queue,
at the place of work, something
like viva, viva mpla was whispered
through the wind-placarded mesh.
And from Paarden Eiland a tick bird cut
north – true as bob, hopes
high, head down, flying
– feet crossed.

A NAMING OF MATCHES

If you twirl a match
in your fingers, it'll
purr like cat:
This one, *Hothead.*
This one, *Firebird.*
This one's tipped with sorrow,
          – *Black Tear.*
This one, *Brazier Warmth.*
This one, *Primus Stove.*
Matches are
          . . . well, straightforward,
you can feel
in the palm of a hand
their honest weight, you can sense
the yellow flower
wrapped in each dark bud . . . .
Strike, Ardent, Toothpick, Piper.
Row upon row in closed ranks they wait
for their baptism of fire.
          This one, *Single.*
          This one, *Spark.*
          This one,
                    Prairie Fire.

LULLABY

But who killed Johannes, mama . . . ?
Sssssssshhh! now close your eyes.
Mama . . . ?
Only a bar of soap, they said.
So *thula, thula,* now quiet my child.

But who killed Solomon, mama . . . ?
Sssssssshhh! your blanket's tucked in.
Who?
Only a length of rope, I suppose.
So *thula, thula,* now quiet my child.

But who killed Ahmed, mama . . . ?
Sssssssshhh! we must get up early.
Please?
Only the tenth floor, I heard.
So *thula, thula,* now quiet my child.

But who killed Joseph, mama . . . ?
Sssssssshhh! tomorrow's work is hard.
Mama . . . ?
Only a flight of stairs, I read.
So *thula, thula,* now quiet my child.

But who killed Steve, mama . . . ?
Sssssssshhh! it's a long walk to the bus.
Mama . . . ?
A brick wall, the magistrate said.
So *thula, thula,* now quiet my child.

But who killed Looksmart, mama . . . ?
Sssssssshhh! sleep and grow strong.
Who, mama . . . ?

His own belt, that's what was blamed.
So *thula, thula,* now quiet my child.

But who . . . .
Thula! Thula! Thula! my child.

A TALE OF WHY TORTOISE CARRIES A HUT UPON HIS BACK

Once long ago, Tortoise challenged a large beast,
saying:
Why do you walk around in this veld
as if it all belonged
exclusively to you?

And the beast replied:
Because I am huge,
because I am great,
because I am called
Tyrranosaurus,
because I have six-inch teeth
I'm destined
for a special, civilising role in this place.

But (just in case)
he made
Tortoise a prisoner and forced him to work
all day, every day, in a field.
Only late afternoons was Tortoise led back
to rest in the quietness of his cell.

Yet often on return he would find
the small world he'd made was smashed,
his few books and letters scattered and awry,
and Tortoise felt anger in his throat
like some, half-swallowed
prehistoric stone.
The bed he'd made was ripped up,
his once folded clothes were scattered on the floor.
The beast had paid yet another visit
while Tortoise was away.

They say Tortoise is a patient one, yes,
he learnt to be by picking up the fragments of a
shattered world
time and time again.

So that's why Tortoise took to carrying
his hut upon his back.
That was long ago.

They tell me Tyrranosaurus is now
extinct,
while Tortoise is alive and well, but you can still see
how he had to stick together broken pieces
– he's got marks on his shell.

CHAMELEON

In your cosmic repose
only the scandal
of two rolling planets betrays your avid
flypaper soul.
Wrapped in technicolour, worked
by fastidious
shifting-spanner toes,
each foot is
lifted slowly
one by
one by one, painstaking
on the track
of flies.

Pinnacle-back, confuser of nature's
metaphysical divides
on the ground evoking
your volcanic beginnings
you become
a stone among stones.
Or you climb up
into the arms of a tree and the tree
blushes
it thinks it has grown a strange
insectivorous leaf.
Last of the fire-breathers,
tongue-in-cheek dragon with your secret
mouthful of rolled-up pink
I have seen you
finally old with age
tiptoe to the end
turn a deep brown and wear
your own death
like another disguise.

KWIKKIE

Pernickety one
. . . quick-step
. . . penny-whistle walk
I like your style
fossicker
pointillist of our yard.
I've studied
your ratchet-work
your seamstress ways
stitch and pulley
I have thought myself
into the flywheel of your clockwork head.
I've watched you long
I know how it feels
to have eyes at the side, or
to end with a beak.

They call me
wagtail now
but actually
        I am cocking my head.

CLOTHES

Shoulder to shoulder with my shirt
I used to move around
Mostly in step with my pants.
We were almost inseparable, once,
Who would have guessed?

First they took my belt away,
Wrist watch, small change,
Later the rest, handed in a packet
To my visitors for safekeeping, and confined

To the same family wardrobe where
I'd hide away as a child, amongst the hush,
Mothballed shoes, cuffs, legs,
Arms, amongst my solemn
Ancestral ranks with their wire
Question marks for heads.

Inside and shutting the door, I'd go to find
How in my supposed absence – ssssh,
The world would sound,

In there. Resolves hardening in the same
Faraway darkness, hanging on unrepentant, it's you now
Listening, you my clothes
Set to confound all our enemies,
Twenty more months now then
We pick up
Where we left off last.

SECOND THOUGHTS

My brother comes on a visit.
The shirt he's wearing looks
Very familiar indeed. The little
Upstart bastard . . . will I really
Ever get back to my clothes?
Or at least, is he who returns
Likely to be remotely the same?
A bit cranky perhaps stronger
Broken down more determined –
All of these things are
At least possibilities, you can't
Mothball yourself. Even in here.
And . . . ?
Okay. Life goes on.
My clothes should be worn.